OS X
Security & Privacy

El Capitan Edition

DIANE YEE

HONU PRESS

OS X Security & Privacy, El Capitan Edition
by Diane Yee

Editor: Bill Gregory
Proofreader: Pat Kissell
Compositor: Birgitte Lund
Cover: Honu Press

Contents

CHAPTER 1

Getting Started

Apple designed OS X with advanced technologies that work together to constantly keep your Mac safe. Some of these features are turned on by default, whereas others are turned off or aren't dialed up to full strength. Some features are front-and-center in System Preferences or the Applications folder, whereas others are buried deep in the user interface. This book covers the whole range of OS X's security and privacy tools and explains the best practices for defending your Mac and data.

Conventions Used in This Book

A shorthand instruction to navigate to a nested folder or to choose a command looks like this:

Choose > System Preferences > Dock > Position on Screen > Left.

Each name between the > symbols refers to an icon, folder, window, dialog box, menu, button, checkbox, option, link, or pane; just look on the screen for a matching label. The refers to the Apple menu, in the top-left corner of the desktop.

Keyboard shortcuts are given in the form "Shift+Command+N".

CHAPTER 2

User Accounts

O S X lets many people use the same computer without being able to see or change each other's files and settings. **User accounts**, which are central to OS X's security, identify who has permission to log in to a particular computer (or network). Like the Unix operating system on which it's based, OS X is designed from the ground up to be a multiple-user operating system. That is, you can set up OS X so that everyone must log in when the computer starts. The > Log Out command summons the login window, as does the accounts menu described in Chapter 6.

To start an OS X session, you log in to your user account: click your own name (or type the first few letters), and type your password (if any). Logging in identifies you uniquely so that OS X can load your personal settings, grant you certain permissions, and take you to the desktop.

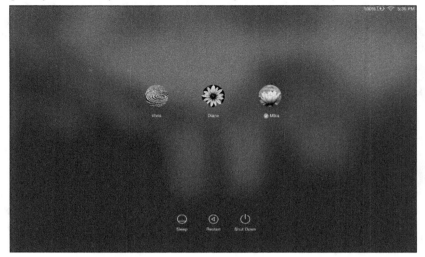

Your user account gives you personalized access to the system. You, like each user, have your own files and settings, including:

- Login items

- Application preferences

- Desktop setup

- System preferences

- Email and internet accounts

- Screen saver

- Apple ID

- iCloud account

- System language

- Files and folders

- Documents

- Internet settings (including bookmarks, home page, history, cookies, and cached webpages)

- User (personal) fonts
- Sharing permissions
- Network connections

Your private files, folders, and preferences generally are stored on the OS X drive in /Users/*user_name*—your **home folder**—which lets OS X personalize your desktop each time that you log in.

On a new computer or during a clean installation, you create the first user account when you set up OS X. If you upgraded from an earlier version of OS X, your existing accounts migrated to the new installation and appear in the login window. If you're on a large network, ask your network administrator how to log in.

Tip: Even if you don't share your Mac and don't create other user accounts, you should still use accounts to password-protect your computer. Turn off automatic login (Chapter 6) to protect your Mac from unauthorized use when you're away from your desk or if your laptop is stolen.

CHAPTER 3

Creating an Account

The Users & Groups panel is the master control center for creating and managing user accounts. To create an account for a new user, choose > System Preferences > Users & Groups > Add button $\boxed{+}$ (click if the settings are dimmed).

The Users & Groups panel lists everyone who has an account. From here, you can create new accounts or change passwords. If you're using a new Mac, there's probably only one account listed here: yours. This account was created automatically when you first installed or set up OS X. You, an administrator, must click to authenticate yourself before you can make changes.

Step 1: Choose an Account Type

OS X offers several types of accounts. When you click $\boxed{+}$ under the list of accounts in Users & Groups, the Create User panel opens. The first step is choosing which type of account to create for the new user.

Administrator Accounts

If this is your own personal Mac, then just under your name on the Users & Groups panel of System Preferences, it probably reads *Admin*, which stands for Administrator.

Because you originally set up OS X, the Mac assumes that you're its **administrator**—the technical person who will maintain this Mac. Only an administrator is allowed to do the following:

- Create accounts on the Mac.

- Create, move, or delete folders outside of your home folder.

- Open, edit, or delete anyone else's files.

- Make changes to certain System Preferences panels, including Date & Time, Energy Saver, Network, and Startup Disk.

- Install new programs into the Applications folder.

- Add fonts that everybody can use.

- Use all features of the Disk Utility program.

- Bypass FileVault (Chapter 12) by using a recovery key.

An administrator has sweeping systemwide rights. You'll find certain settings all over OS X that you can change *only* if you're an administrator—including many in the Users & Groups panel itself. Administrator status is also required when you want to network your Mac to other kinds of computers.

As you create accounts for other people who'll use your Mac, you can make each one an administrator too. Use discretion. Only trustworthy and technically savvy people should be granted administrative rights.

Standard Accounts

Most people, on most Macs, are ordinary **Standard** account holders. A Standard account has access only to its own home folder and to shared folders (Chapter 8). Standard users can change settings related to only their own accounts (picture, password, and desktop preferences, for example) and install programs and fonts for only their own use. Most other areas of the Mac are off limits.

Tip: Some System Preferences panels display a lock icon 🔒. If you're a Standard account holder, then you can't make changes to these settings without the help of an administrator. Fortunately, you don't have to log out so that an administrator can log in and make changes. Instead, call the admin over, click the lock icon, and let him type his name and password (provided he feels comfortable letting you make the changes).

Managed Accounts with Parental Controls

A **Managed** account is the same as a Standard user but with additional usage limits set by an administrator using Parental Controls (Chapter 4). You can turn a Managed account into a Standard account by turning off Parental Controls, and vice versa. Use a Managed account for children or anyone else you don't quite trust.

Sharing Only Account

This type of account is especially useful if your Mac is on a network.

Ordinarily, you can log in and access the files on your Mac either in person (seated in front of it) or from across the network. This restrictive arrangement was designed for situations where many people share a *single* Mac (families and schools, for example) but is clumsy and ponderous when the people on a home or office network each have their *own* computers. If your spouse or coworker wanted to copy files from you, you'd have to create accounts for them on *your* Mac, complete with superfluous home folders that they'd never use.

The **Sharing Only** account solves this problem: this account can access the Mac *only* remotely (over a network) to share files. It has no home folder, can't change settings or log in via the login window, and can't turn on FileVault (Chapter 12). A Sharing Only account exists solely for the purpose of file sharing on the network, and people can enter their names and passwords only from other Macs.

Group

A **group** is a virtual container that holds the names of other account holders. You might create one for coworkers on your team or children in your household, for example. Groups streamline file-sharing privileges (Chapter 8), making it easy to change permissions settings on a networked Mac, or a Mac with many account holders.

In the Users & Groups panel, click ⊞ and then select Group from the New Account pop-up menu. Type a name for the new group (Marketing, Children, or whatever) and then click Create Group. In the list that opens, select the checkboxes of the accounts that you want to be members of the group.

You can create as many groups as you like, and each account can belong to multiple groups (or no group). Later, to share a folder or file, you can save time by choosing a group name instead of setting account permissions individually.

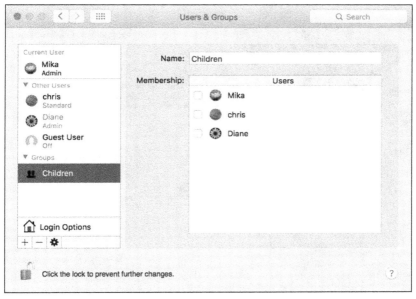

The Guest Account

The **Guest** account (there's only one) is for temporary, passwordless logins and is intended for visitors, friends, and transients who want to use your Mac for just a while. When the guest logs out, the account is reset and all its files, email, browser history, and settings are erased from your Mac.

The Guest account isn't listed among the account types in the New Account pop-up menu. To enable the Guest account, choose > System Preferences > Users & Groups (click 🔒 if the settings are dimmed). Select Guest User and then select "Allow guests to log in to this computer". You can also apply Parental Controls (Chapter 4) and prevent guests from using shared folders (Chapter 8).

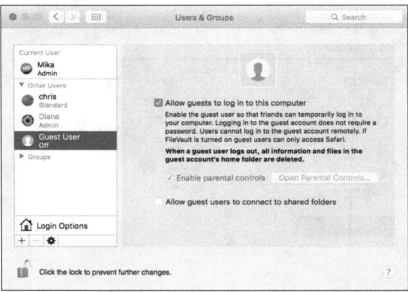

Step 2: Set the Name and Password

After choosing the account type (page 8), specify the following information about the new account holder in the Create User panel:

Full Name
> The full name typically is the name of a person (first, last, or both names) but can be any word(s). You can change the full name after creating the account.

Account Name
> OS X proposes a **short name** but you can change it to any word without spaces or punctuation. The login window lets you use your full or short name, but network and dial-up connections require a short name. The user's home folder is labeled with the short name. You can't easily change this name after creating the account (see "Advanced Account Options" on page 36).

Password

Choose whether to log in to OS X by using the same password as an iCloud account (so you have to remember only one password), or by using a separate, independent password. If you choose "Use iCloud password", then an internet connection is required to authenticate the iCloud password the first time that the user logs in.

Tip: Use an **Apple ID** (*appleid.apple.com*) for your iCloud Account. Your Apple ID identifies you uniquely for Apple.com store transactions, iTunes Store, App Store, iBooks Store, Messages, AirDrop, iCloud, Apple retail store reservations, and Apple.com support. An Apple ID requires a valid email address to register. Use a personal address that you anticipate having for a long time (such as a Gmail or Yahoo email address); don't use your work or school email address.

---

iCloud ID (if "Use iCloud password" is selected)

Type the email address used for the user's iCloud ID.

Required, Verify (if "Use separate password" is selected)

Type and then retype the user's password, or leave both fields empty for a passwordless account. To get password advice, click 🔑 (Chapter 14).

Hint (if "Use separate password" is selected)

Type an (optional) memory-jogging hint for the password. (All users can see this hint.) The login window shows hints only if they're enabled in Login Options (Chapter 6).

Click the "Create User" button and then complete the following options in the Password pane. The available options depend on your account type (Administrator, Standard, and so on) and whether you're changing your own account or someone else's.

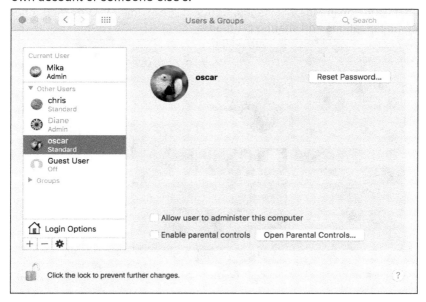

Picture
See "Step 3: Choose a Picture" on page 16.

Change Password/Reset Password
Change the user's login password and password hint.

Contacts Card
View or edit the user's Contacts entry (if available).

Allow user to reset password using Apple ID
Lets the user reset a forgotten password after entering an Apple ID. See "Forgotten Passwords" on page 44.

Allow user to administer this computer
Gives a Standard or Managed user administrative rights.

Enable parental controls
Adds Parental Controls (Chapter 4) restrictions to Standard accounts.

Login Items
See "Step 4: Choose Login Items (Startup Items)" on page 18.

Step 3: Choose a Picture

The login window displays each account holder's name, accompanied by a small picture. This picture is not only your icon on the login window, but also your icon in Mail, Messages, Contacts, FaceTime, AirDrop, and other communications and sharing programs.

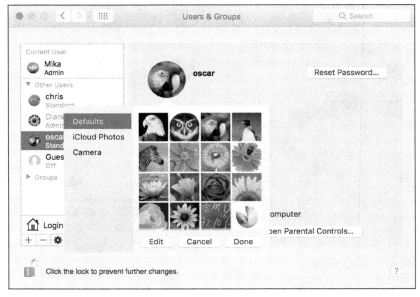

To choose your own picture:

- **Drag and drop.** Drag and drop an image file from the Finder onto the user picture.

- **Use an existing picture.** Click the user picture, click a category, and then select a picture. Click Done to add your account image.

  - ▶ Defaults: Pictures that are included with OS X.

  - ▶ Recents: Pictures that were recently used as user pictures.

  - ▶ My Photo Stream: Pictures from your photo stream (the last 1000 photos you've taken with, or imported into, your Mac).

  - ▶ iCloud Photos: Pictures from iCloud, available if iCloud Photo Library is turned on in iCloud preferences.

  - ▶ Faces: Faces recognized in your photos.

  - ▶ Linked: Picture from Contacts.

- **Snap a photo.** To take a new picture with your computer's built-in camera, click the user picture, click Camera, and then click the camera button. After a countdown of three seconds, the camera takes your picture. Click Done to add your account image.

Tip: To frame a picture properly, click the picture and then drag the cropping slider under the picture.

Step 4: Choose Login Items (Startup Items)

Account holders can specify any programs, documents, drives, network servers, files, or folders to open automatically at log in. (This setting is available only to whoever is currently logged in—an administrator can't set login items for other people.)

To choose your login items, choose > System Preferences > Users & Groups (click if the settings are dimmed). Click your account and then click the Login Items tab.

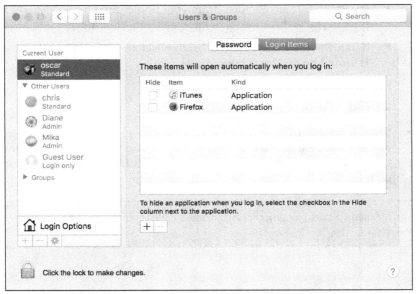

You can add any icon to the list of items that you want to start automatically. Click + to display the Open dialog box, where you can navigate to the icon, select it, and then click Choose. Alternatively, if you can see the icon in a folder window or on the desktop, then drag it into the list. To remove an item, click it in the list and then click −. You can also turn on the Hide checkbox for each item so that the program runs in the background after login, ready to be summoned with a click.

Tip: To add a program to the Login Items list quickly, right-click (or two-finger tap) its dock icon and then choose Options > Open at Login.

CHAPTER 4

Parental Controls

If you're setting up a Standard or Managed account, the Parental Controls checkbox lets you shield your Mac from harm done by young, naive, overwhelmed, or not-entirely-trustworthy users—particularly young children, students, and older adults. (Parental Controls is also available for Administrator accounts, but you normally wouldn't grant admin rights to such a person, and OS X will display a message to this effect if you apply Parental Controls to an Administrator account.)

You can set limits on programs run (including games played), Safari website access, Mail communications, login hours, and more. You can also log a user's activities for later review.

Tip: If you apply Parental Controls to a Standard account, then the account type listed on the Users & Groups panel changes from Standard to Managed.

To set up Parental Controls for an account, choose > System Preferences > Parental Controls. If necessary, click to unlock the settings. Select the account in the list and then click Enable Parental Controls. Set the desired restrictions in each tab (Apps, Web, and so on). To turn off all settings, click > Turn off Parental Controls.

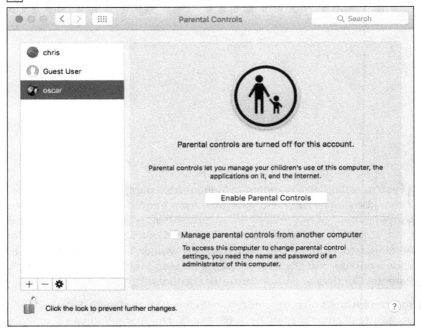

Apps Tab

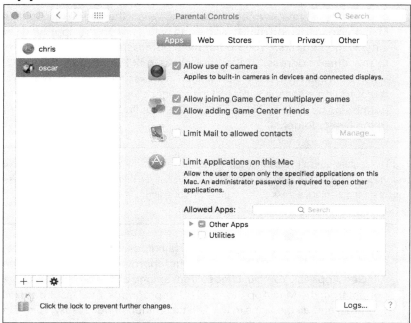

The Apps tab limits which programs and features the Managed account holder can use. These settings are especially useful for shared-computer situations like classrooms, where peer pressure can lead to temptation when you're not looking.

The following restrictions are available:

- To forbid the use of the Mac's camera for taking selfies or making video calls with, say, FaceTime or Skype, clear "Allow use of camera". The Mac's built-in camera and cameras on connected external displays are disabled.

- To limit access to Apple's online multiplayer social gaming network, select the desired Game Center checkboxes. You can prevent the user from playing multiplayer games in Game Center, or prevent the user from sending and receiving friend requests in Game Center.

- To limit the exchange of email to a list of approved people, select "Limit Mail to allowed contacts", click Manage, and then create a list of approved contacts. To edit the list, click $+$ or $-$, or drag cards to the list from the Contacts app. When the user opens Mail, the contacts list is empty except for the people you've approved.

To receive email notifications when the user tries to exchange email with an unapproved contact, click Manage, turn on "Send requests to", and then type your own email address. When the user uses Apple's Mail program to send mail to someone who's *not* on the approved list a message appears: "You do not have permission to send messages to this email address." If the user clicks Ask Permission, then *your* email address receives a permission-request message; meanwhile, the outgoing message is placed in the user's Drafts folder. If you grant permission by clicking Always Allow, the user finds out on the next visit to the Drafts folder.

Tip: This feature doesn't stop email using *other* programs, such as Microsoft Outlook, or web-based email such as Google Gmail or Yahoo Mail. If you think that the user will bypass your restrictions, block access to those programs by using "Limit Applications on this Mac" (described next) or websites by using the Web tab.

- To prevent the user from opening certain apps, select "Limit Applications on this Mac", and then select the approved applications in the Allowed Apps list. You can choose from among all the programs you've bought from the Mac App Store, all other programs, the Dashboard (all widgets), and all the apps in the Utilities folder. (If necessary, click the tiny triangles to expand the list.) Only selected items will appear in the account holder's Applications folder. If you don't see a program listed, then use the search box, or drag its icon from a Finder window to the list.

Web Tab

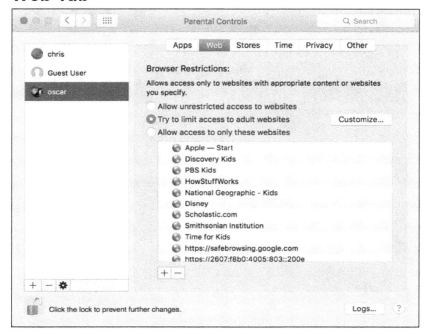

The Web tab limits which websites the user is allowed to visit.

Three levels of filtering are available, from least to most restrictive:

- **Allow unrestricted access to websites.** No filtering. The user can roam the web freely.

- **Try to limit access to adult websites.** OS X analyzes the content of each website before displaying it in Safari and then filters (suppresses) any sites that contain adult material. The filtering rules are hardly flawless. To override the filters on a per-site basis, click Customize and then edit the "Always allow" and "Never allow" lists.

- **Allow access to only these websites.** Create a **whitelist** of the only websites that the user is allowed to visit. The list comes pre-loaded with kid-friendly sites (Apple, Disney, and so on). To edit the list, click ⊞ and ⊟.

Stores Tab

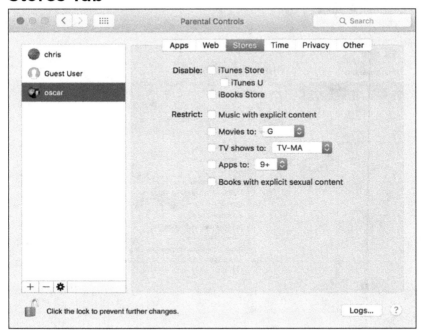

The Stores tab disables access to the iTunes Store, iTunes U, and the iBooks Store, and limits access to music, movies, TV shows, apps, and books to only those with age-appropriate ratings (the available ratings vary by country and media type).

Time Tab

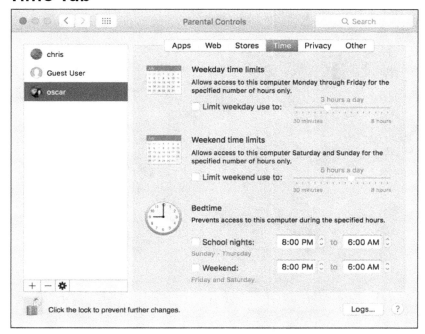

The Time tab limits the number of hours, and which hours, the user can use the Mac. A user who tries to log in outside the time limits that you specify is stonewalled with the message, "Computer time expired". The user can request additional time, from 15 minutes to "Rest of the day", with an administrator's consent (password). Similarly, as the user's allotted time on the Mac winds down, the message, "Your computer time is almost up" appears. Again, an admin can grant more time.

You can specify:

- **How much time.** In the "Weekday time limits" and "Weekend time limits" sections, turn on "Limit weekday use to" or "Limit weekend use to" and then adjust the sliders.

- **Which hours.** In the "Bedtime" section, turn on the checkbox for either "School nights" or "Weekend", and then set the hours of the day when the Mac is unavailable to the user.

Tip: When time limits have been set, the user can check how much Mac time remains by clicking the menu-bar clock (which displays the current time). A menu opens with an item that reads, for example, "Parental Controls: Time Remaining 2:36".

Privacy Tab

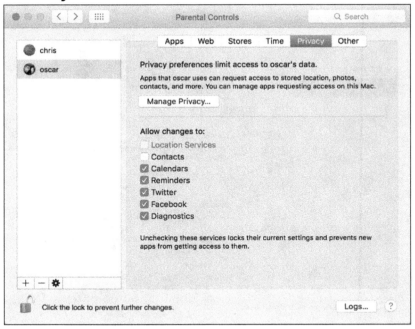

The Privacy tab limits the privacy-related changes that the user can make.

To restrict the user's personal information that the Mac makes available to others on the internet or on a network, click Manage Privacy to open the Privacy pane of Security & Privacy preferences. For details, see Chapter 16.

To let the user control privacy-related changes, select any of the apps or services in the "Allow changes to" list. If the user is prompted by an app to access contacts, for example, and the Contacts checkbox isn't selected, then the user can't allow or forbid access (the current administrator setting is used). If the Contacts checkbox is selected, then the user can allow or forbid access.

Other Tab

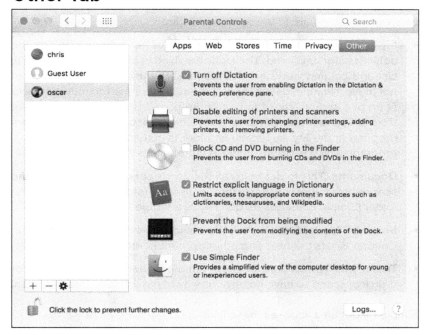

The Other tab contains miscellaneous options:

- **Turn off Dictation.** Prevents the user from dictating text instead of typing on the keyboard.

- **Disable editing of printers and scanners.** Prevents the user from deleting or installing printers or editing printer settings.

- **Block CD and DVD burning in the Finder.** Prevents the user from using Finder to burn CDs or DVDs (other disc-burning apps still work).

- **Restrict explicit language in Dictionary.** Prevents profanity from appearing in OS X's built-in unabridged The New Oxford American Dictionary.

- **Prevent the Dock from being modified.** Prevents the user from changing the icons in the dock.

Use Simple Finder

If you're especially concerned about a person's profound negligence or lack of computer skills, turn on Use Simple Finder.

Simple Finder presents the user with a stripped-down desktop: only four menus (, Finder, File, and Help), no drive icon, and a minimal dock. The only visible folders are in the dock, and include:

- **My Applications.** This folder holds icons of the applications that the administrator approved. The icons are fixed in place in a uniform grid. List and column views aren't available. The user can click icons but not move, rename, delete, or sort them. If there are too many icons to fit on one screen, click the numbered page buttons at the bottom of the window to move from one set of icons to another. (Note that every program in the My Applications folder is actually an alias to the real program, which is stored safely in the off-limits Applications folder.)

- **Documents.** This folder holds all the user's personal files. Behind the scenes, this folder is actually the Documents folder in the user's home folder (Simple Finder users don't have a visible home folder).

- **Shared.** This folder, which is the same Shared folder described in Chapter 8, lets the user and other account holders exchange files.

- **Trash.** The Trash is only for show. Simple Finder users can't select or drag icons, and so have no obvious way to put anything into the Trash.

Simple Finder also imposes these limits:

- Finder is the only program with its icon on the dock.

- One click (not two) opens an icon.

- Folders can't be created.

- The menu has only the Log Out, Force Quit, and Sleep commands.

- The Finder menu has only the About Finder, Run Full Finder, and Services commands. The Services command lets the user edit keyboard shortcuts. The Run Full Finder command prompts the user for an administrator's user name and password, and then restores the normal Finder. To return to Simple Finder, choose Finder > Return to Simple Finder.

- The File menu has only the Close Window command.

- Spotlight search isn't available.

Tip: Simple Finder doesn't restrict or change any administrator-approved application. A program running inside Simple Finder keeps all its features and normal behaviors.

Logging the User's Activities

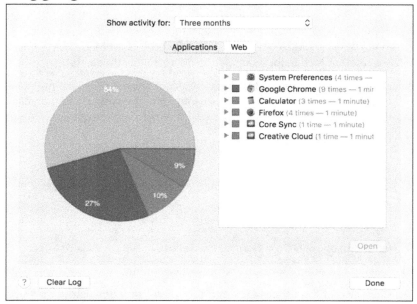

The Logs feature records the user's activities for your later review. To view the logs, click Logs at the bottom of the Parental Controls panel and then click one of the tabs (Applications or Web).

- The Applications log lists which programs the user opened (or tried to open). The list is sorted from most-used to least-used, as illustrated by the accompanying interactive pie chart showing the percentage of time spent in each app. Click the tiny triangle next to a program name in the list to see time, date, and duration details.

- The Web log lists which websites the user visited (or tried to visit). The list is sorted from most-used to least-used, as illustrated by the accompanying interactive pie chart showing the percentage of time spent at each website. Click the tiny triangle next to a website or webpage name in the list to see time and date details.

To block the user from using an app or visiting a website, select it in the list and then click Restrict. To unblock the app or website, click Allow. To open the selected app or website, click Open.

Use the "Show activity for" pop-up menu to change the time period being reported (today, three months, or whatever).

To erase the history of either the Applications log or Web log, click Clear Log.

Remote Parental Controls

Parental Controls are useful in environments where multiple Macs on the same network are in use (in classrooms or crowded households, for example). You can adjust Parental Controls settings for Macs 1, 2, 3, and 4 while seated at Mac 5, for example. To do so, follow these steps:

1   Log in to the first remote Mac (not your Mac), choose > System Preferences > Parental Controls, click , enter your password, and then click the name of the account that you want to manage remotely.

2   Click > Allow Remote Setup.

3   Close System Preferences.

4   Repeat steps 1–3 for each account on each Mac on the network that you want to manage remotely.

5   Return to *your* Mac.

6   In Finder, choose Go > Connect to Server, and then click Browse.

    A list of the other Macs on the network appears.

7   Click one of the other Macs and then enter an administrator's name and password for that Mac.

8   Choose > System Preferences > Parental Controls, click , and then enter your password.

    A section named Other Computers appears in the Users & Groups list.

9   Click the account name (on the other Mac) whose Parental Controls settings you want to change remotely and then enter the administrator name and password of the remote computer.

10 Repeat steps 6–9 for the other Macs and accounts that you want to manage remotely.

CHAPTER 5

Editing Accounts

If you're an administrator, you can change your own account in any way that you like. If you have any other kind of account, however, you can change only your picture, password, Apple ID, and login items (Chapter 3). To make any other changes, you must ask an admin to log in, make the desired changes to your account, and then turn the computer back to you.

Deleting Accounts

To delete an account from your Mac, choose ⬤ > System Preferences > Users & Groups. Click the account name in the accounts list and then click ☐ under the list. OS X asks what to do with all the user's files and settings:

- **Save the home folder in a disk image.** OS X preserves the deleted account holder's folders on the Mac, in a single, space-saving archive that can be reopened in case it's needed again.

  The disk image file (.dmg) lands in the /Users/Deleted Users folder. If you double-click it, a new, virtual disk icon named for the deleted account appears on your desktop. You can open folders and treat it as if it were an actual home folder.

  If the person ever returns, you can use this disk image to reinstate the deleted user's account: create a new account and then copy the contents of the folders in the mounted disk image (Documents, Pictures, Desktop, and so on) into the corresponding folders of the new home folder.

- **Don't change the home folder.** OS X removes the *account* from the login window and the Users & Groups panel of System Preferences, but leaves the *home folder* untouched. Use this option if you don't want to delete the user's files just yet.

- **Delete the home folder.** The account and all its files and settings are deleted forever. The "Erase home folder securely" option overwrites the drive space where the home folder was with meaningless data, so that deleted files can't be undeleted with specialized data-recovery tools.

Tip: If you delete a Sharing Only account (page 10), OS X won't ask whether to preserve the home folder because a Sharing Only account has no home folder.

CHAPTER 6

Setting Up the Login Process

After you've set up more than one account, the login window appears whenever:

- You turn on the Mac

- You choose > Log Out

- The Mac logs you out automatically

You, an administrator, can set additional options that can tighten or reduce security at the login window (more secure = less convenient). Choose > System Preferences > Users & Groups, click , enter an administrator password, click Login Options, and then set the desired options:

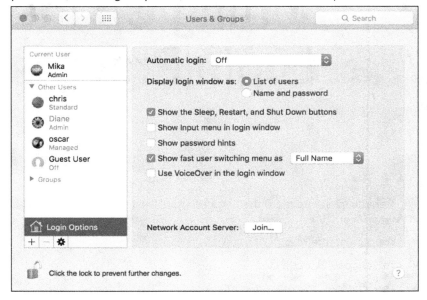

- **Automatic login.** Enable automatic login for a specific user (more convenient) or force all users to log in (more secure). Automatic login works best if only one person uses the Mac, or uses it most of the time. When auto-login is turned on, startup bypasses the login window and shows the specified user's desktop automatically. Other users still can use their accounts via fast user switching or when the user logs out (> Log Out). This option is convenient but insecure because anyone can log in just by turning on the computer.

- **Display login window as.** The "List of users" option (more convenient) shows a list of user names and pictures in the login window. The "Name and password" option (more secure) hides the pictures and makes every user type a name and password.

- **Show the Sleep, Restart, and Shut Down buttons.** Choose whether to show these buttons in the login window (more convenient) or hide them (more secure). A technically savvy enemy can circumvent OS X security by bypassing the login window during a restart (restarting at the Unix Terminal or in target disk mode, for example). Turning off this option adds a modest layer of security, but for strong security, use FileVault (Chapter 12) or set a firmware password (page 38).

- **Show Input menu in login window.** Choose whether to let users select a keyboard language in the login window. Turn on this option if the Mac's various account holders speak different languages or use different keyboard layouts and alphabets.

- **Show password hints.** Choose whether to let users see their password hints set in Users & Groups. OS X displays a password hint on the login window at the user's request. If this option is turned off, then hints don't appear (which adds a layer of security, depending on how obvious the hints are).

- **Show fast user switching menu as.** Choose whether simultaneous logins are allowed. Fast user switching lets multiple users stay logged in at the same time. You can leave your programs running and documents open securely and invisibly in the background while someone else logs in. When you switch back to your account, OS X resumes your session where you left off. If fast user switching is turned on, the **accounts menu** appears on the right side of the menu bar, listing all the account holders on the computer. Use the pop-up menu to show the accounts menu as a user name or a compact icon.

- **Use VoiceOver in the login window.** Choose whether to have VoiceOver speak the parts of the login window (for blind users).

- **Network Account Server.** If you're on a large network, your network administrator will tell you how to connect to an open directory server, active directory domain, or OS X Server.

Tip: You can create an "If found, contact…" message that always appears in the login window: choose > System Preferences > Security & Privacy > General (click if the settings are dimmed). Turn on "Show a message when the screen is locked", click Set Lock Message, and then type your message (press Option+Return to create a new paragraph).

Advanced Account Options

As an administrator, you can't easily *change* your account's short name (the account name (page 13), as opposed to the full name) that you created originally, but you can create *another* one that works equally well when you log in or authenticate yourself.

1   Choose > System Preferences > Users & Groups.

2   Right-click (or two-finger tap) the account name in the accounts list and then choose Advanced Options in the shortcut menu.

The Advanced Options panel opens.

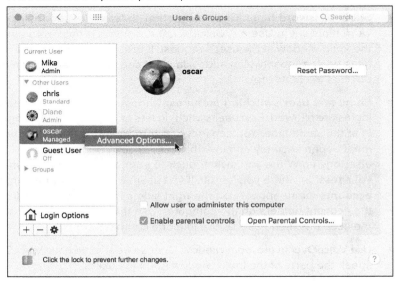

3 Click $\boxed{+}$ under the Aliases list, type an alternative account (short) name, and then click OK.

You can create as many of these aliases as you like.

Tip: Don't edit the "Account name" box in the Advanced Options panel; it won't work.

4 Click OK.

The next time you log in to your Mac, you can use your new short name instead of the old one.

Firmware Passwords

If you haven't turned on FileVault (Chapter 12), a clever enemy can bypass all OS X's security features in a few seconds by using Unix console commands, single-user mode, FireWire disk mode, and other tricks. Fortunately, you can secure your Mac completely by turning on the firmware password.

1   Restart your Mac while holding down Command+R.

    OS X's Recovery console starts.

2   Choose your language.

3   Choose Utilities > Firmware Password Utility.

4   Enter an administrator's password.

5   Turn on "Require password to change firmware settings".

6   Create a firmware password. This password will be required to start your Mac from anything but the normal internal system drive.

7   Enter an administrator's password. A message tells you, "The settings were successfully saved".

8   Restart your Mac.

From now on, whenever you (or anybody) starts your Mac in anything other than the normal way, the firmware password is required. The following startup methods, for example, all require the firmware password:

- Holding down Shift to start in Safe Mode, or holding down Command+V to start in verbose mode.

- Holding down Option to start from a different system drive, or holding down X to start from an alternate startup drive.

- Holding down C to start from a bootable CD, DVD, or USB drive.

- Holding down D or Option+D to start Apple Hardware Test or Apple Diagnostics.

- Holding down N or Option+N to start from a NetBoot server.

- Holding down Command+R or Command+Option+R to start from OS X Recovery.

- Holding down Command+Option+P+R to reset NVRAM.

- Holding down Command+S to start in single-user mode.

- Holding down T to start in target disk mode.

CHAPTER 7

Logging In and Out

Logging in starts your session in OS X. **Logging out** ends the session and prevents others from accessing your files and settings.

Logging In

After you start your Mac or the preceding user chooses > Log Out, the login window appears. You can proceed in any of several ways:

- **Restart.** You can restart your computer to troubleshoot or complete a software update. If you restart or shut down, OS X prompts you to save any unsaved work. (The Restart and Shut Down buttons don't appear here if an administrator has hidden them as a security precaution; see Chapter 6.)

- **Shut Down.** Shutting down powers off the computer (if you have a laptop, wait for it to shut down completely before closing the lid).

- **Log In.** Logging in identifies you uniquely so that OS X can load your personal settings, grant you certain permissions, and take you to your desktop the way you last left it (or the way an administrator set it up for you). To log in, click your name (or type it if there's no user list), type your password if prompted, and then press Return or click the arrow icon in the password box. In a long list, use the arrow keys to scroll to your name or type its first few letters. If you click the wrong person's name accidentally, click Back.

  The password box shakes if you type the wrong password: correct it or click the question mark in the password box to show your password hint (if you've set one in Users & Groups). Passwords are case-sensitive; ⇪ appears in the password box if Caps Lock is on. By default, you can mistype your password an unlimited number of times. If you forget your password, see "Forgotten Passwords" on page 44.

Tip: If you're not an administrator, then you're not allowed to install any new programs (or to put anything else) into the Applications folder. This folder (and a few others) is used by every account holder on the Mac. Nonadministrators can't move or change universally shared folders.

Logging Out

When you log out, OS X disconnects your online connections and prevents others from using your user account to access your files or network. Programs that don't use Auto Save prompt you to save any unsaved work. Your computer remains turned on and OS X shows the login window to let the next person log in.

- **To log out after a cancelable delay.** Choose > Log Out (or press Shift+Command+Q).

- **To log out immediately.** Hold down the Option key and then choose > Log Out (or press Shift+Option+Command+Q).

- **To log out automatically after an idle period.** Choose > System Preferences > Security & Privacy (click if the settings are dimmed). Click the Advanced button and then select "Log out after _ minutes of inactivity".

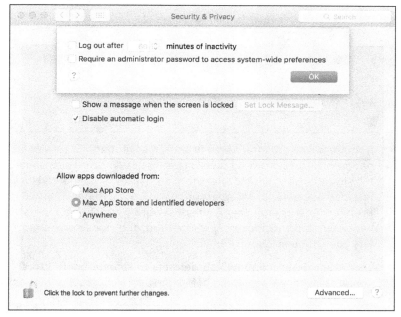

Logout Options

To increase security and set other logout options, choose > System Preferences > Security & Privacy > General.

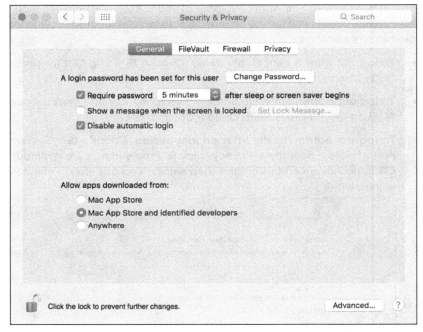

- **Require password after sleep or screen saver begins.** Turning on this option locks (password-protects) the screensaver. Whenever somebody tries to wake up your Mac after the screensaver has appeared (or when the Mac has gone to sleep according to your settings in > System Preferences > Energy Saver), the password dialog box appears. If fast user switching (Chapter 9) is enabled, the password dialog box lets you choose a user when you unlock.

  Use the pop-up menu (which defaults to "immediately") to set the amount of time that must pass before the password requirement kicks in.

Tip: You can use a Terminal command to specify any time interval (not only the pre-set menu choices): `defaults -currentHost write com.apple.screensaver askForPasswordDelay -int` *interval*, where *interval* specifies the number of seconds to wait before a password is required.

- **Show a message when the screen is locked.** Use this option to add a personal message ("Back in 5 minutes " or your mobile number, for example) to the login window and screensaver.

- **Disable automatic login.** To require logins for all users, turn on this option. This option duplicates the "Automatic login" checkbox described in Chapter 6.

To set additional logout options, click the Advanced button at the bottom of the Security & Privacy panel:

- **Log out after _ minutes of inactivity.** Use this option to log out and show the login window automatically after an idle period of not touching the mouse, keyboard, or trackpad (when you wander off without explicitly logging out, for example).

- **Require an administrator password to access system-wide preferences.** Normally, only administrators can change System Preferences that affect the entire computer and everyone who uses it (Date & Time, Users & Groups, Network, and Security & Privacy, for example). A nonadministrator can change these secure preferences only if an administrator clicks 🔒 and enters a name and password to approve the changes. Unlocking any *one* System Preferences panel, however, unlocks them *all*, and the user can keep making changes without the administrator's knowledge. To require an administrator to unlock each System Preferences panel individually, turn on this option.

Forgotten Passwords

You forgot your login password.

If you're not an administrator (or if you are one but there's another adminis-trator account), then the administrator can choose > System Preferences > Users & Groups, click your account name, and then click Reset Password.

If you're the only administrator, you have several options, provided you turned them on in advance:

- **Password hint.** Show the password hint that you set in > Prefer-ences > Users & Groups. The login window shows hints only if they're enabled in Login Options (Chapter 6).

- **Apple ID.** If "Allow user to reset password using Apple ID" was previ-ously turned on in > System Preferences > Users & Groups, then you can click the question mark in the password box when you're logging in. A message appears: "If you forgot your password, you can reset it using your Apple ID". Click → to open the Reset Password dialog box. Enter your Apple ID and password and then click Reset Password. A message appears telling you that changing your account password creates a new keychain (Chapter 15). (The old keychain remains and can be unlocked if you remember your old password.) Click OK. Enter a new password (twice) and password hint, and then click Reset Password. Click Continue Log In to log in with your new password.

- **FileVault recovery key.** If FileVault (Chapter 12) is turned on, then you can use your recovery key (an emergency master password) to log in. (If you opted to store the recovery key with Apple, then call Apple tech support; they'll give it to you.) Restart the Mac. On the login window, click your name, click the question mark, and then click "Reset it using your Recovery Key", and then type your recovery key.

CHAPTER 8

Sharing Across Accounts

Every account holder has a private home folder (all in the Users folder on the OS X system drive). You can't open any other user's home folder and drop files in it—if you try, you'll see a tiny red "off-limits" icon ⊘ superimposed on almost every folder inside. Fortunately, OS X offers other ways for people to share files and folders across accounts.

The Shared Folder

The Shared folder is in the Users folder on the system drive. The Shared folder is a single folder available to every account on the Mac (it doesn't belong to any particular user). Each user, administrator or not, can add, open, or delete files in the Shared folder without restriction.

Tip: If your family members all share the same Mac but have different accounts, and you all want to listen to the same music collection (MP3 files) by using the iTunes application, then move all the audio files into a new folder (named Music or whatever) and then move that music folder into the Shared folder, where it's available to everybody. Each account holder can log in, open iTunes, choose iTunes > Preferences > Advanced, and then click Change to choose the shared music folder.

The Public Folder

The easiest way to share files is to put them in your Public folder. Everyone with a user account on your Mac or on the same network can access your Public folder, no password needed. You can't choose who can access it—either everyone can or no one can. You must move or copy files to the Public folder—aliases won't work. Every user account has its own Public folder in its home folder. To share your Public folder, choose > System Preferences > Sharing and then select the File Sharing checkbox. All files and folders that you put in your Public folder become available to all users locally and over the network.

The Drop Box

The Drop Box folder, located within your Public folder, lets others securely give *you* files. People can drop files and folders into your Drop Box, but they can't actually open it. This folder, too, is available both locally and over the network. (Don't confuse the Drop Box folder with the online Dropbox service.)

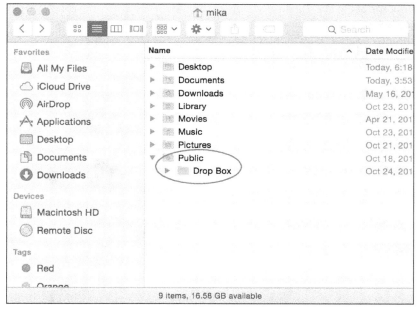

AirDrop

AirDrop lets you quickly and wirelessly send files to other nearby AirDrop users on Macs and iOS devices, without any setup, passwords, special settings, or base stations. To see other people nearby who are using Air-Drop, click the AirDrop icon in the sidebar of any Finder window (or press Shift+Command+R). The user pictures and computer names of those near you appear in the AirDrop window. To share a file with someone, drag it to that person's picture. After the person accepts the file, it's transferred directly to their Downloads folder. When you're done sharing, close the AirDrop (Finder) window to make your Mac invisible to others.

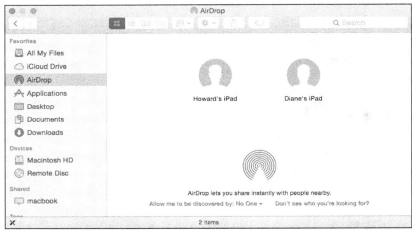

AirDrop encrypts files for transfer and creates a private firewall between you and the other person. AirDrop can also use an Apple ID to verify the identity of the person trying to send you a file. If senders are in your Contacts list and are signed in with their Apple IDs, their names will appear under their photos in AirDrop. To cancel an incoming transfer, open the Downloads folder or stack and then click the × that appears on the icon. AirDrop uses wi-fi to transfer files (to turn on wi-fi, choose > System Preferences > Network > Wi-Fi > Turn Wi-Fi On).

When you use AirDrop to send a file between two devices that have the same Apple ID, the file is downloaded automatically on the receiving device, making it easy to transfer files between two of your own devices.

Tip: You can receive files even when AirDrop isn't selected in Finder. You can choose to make yourself available to only your Contacts or to everyone. When a file is sent to you, it appears as a notification. Click to download the file.

Any-Folder Sharing

Using the Public folder can be inefficient. If you're sharing hundreds of photos, for example, it's wasteful to store copies in both your (unshared) Pictures folder and your Public folder. If you create or update files frequently, it's cumbersome to keep copying them to your Public folder.

Use any-folder sharing to share files and folders directly from the location where they're stored (typically, in your Documents, Pictures, or Music folder). You can set sharing permissions for individual users rather than for everyone on your network, giving some people more or less access (or no access).

To share any folder by using the Info window: Choose > System Preferences > Sharing and then select the File Sharing checkbox.

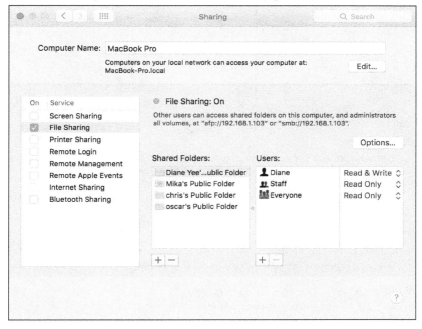

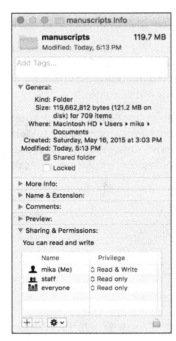

In Finder, select the folder or drive that you want to share and then choose File > Get Info (Command+I). In the Info window, expand the General panel and then select "Shared Folder". (Type your administrator password, if prompted.) Expand the Sharing & Permissions panel (click 🔒 if the settings are dimmed).

Select an existing user or group. Or add a new user: click ⎡+⎤, click New Person, type a name and password for the account, click Create Account, select the user in the list, and then click Select. To add an address-book contact, click Contacts, select the contact, click Select, assign a password to the new sharing account, and then click Create Account.

To choose a permission for yourself or another user, select from the pop-up menus in the Privilege column:

Read & Write
Lets a user add or delete a file, or open a file and change its contents.

Read Only
Lets a user open a file to see or copy its contents, but not change, move, or delete the original file.

Write only (Drop Box)
Lets a user copy files to the shared folder, but not see or change the folder's contents. Only the drop box's owner can open it to take out files.

No Access (available only to "everyone")
Blocks all access. Users can see the folder or drive icon but can't open, change, or copy it.

To apply the same permissions to every item contained in the selected folder or drive, click ⚙▾ > "Apply to enclosed items".

To change the item's owner, select the new owner in the Name column, and then click ⚙▾ > "Make '*name*' the owner".

To remove a user or group, select the user or group in the Name column, and then click —. The entry Everyone refers to everyone who's not specifically listed in the Name column.

To share any folder by using the Sharing preferences panel: Choose > System Preferences > Sharing and then select the File Sharing checkbox. The permissions table works the same way as it does in the Info window, except that the extra column, Shared Folders, shows all shared folders and drives in a master list (you can drag items from the desktop or a Finder window to this list). Use the + — buttons to add and delete folders and users in the list (you can also turn off sharing for Public folders here).

To share with Windows users: Choose > System Preferences > Sharing, and then select the File Sharing checkbox. Click Options and then select "Share files and folders using SMB". (Windows uses the SMB—Server Message Block—protocol). Select the On checkbox for each account that will share files with a Windows computer.

To connect to a shared folder: In a Finder window, choose Go > Network (Shift+Command+K) to show the computers that you can access. To connect as a registered user, select the computer's icon, and then click Connect As in the connection bar near the top of the window. (Alternatively, you can connect as a no-login guest to access only Public folders.) Double-click a computer icon or click its name in the sidebar (if necessary, choose Finder > Preferences > Sidebar, and then select items under Shared). Use shared drives, folders, and files as you would any other Finder items (subject to their read–write permissions). To disconnect from a computer, click ⏏ next to its name in the Finder sidebar. To connect to an internet or unlisted server (by, say, WebDAV, DNS, NFS, FTP, or IP address), choose Go > Connect to Server (Command+K). You can also navigate to shares from within the Save and Open dialog boxes. To wake a sleeping computer for network access, choose > System Preferences > Energy Saver.

To get information about or troubleshoot a network: Choose Applications > Utilities > Network Utility.

CHAPTER 9

Fast User Switching

Fast user switching lets multiple users stay logged in at the same time. You can leave your programs running and documents open securely and invisibly in the background while someone else logs in. When you switch back to your account, OS X resumes your session where you left off. Fast user switching is handy when you're logged in, and someone else wants to use the computer for a moment to check email or a calendar. Depending on how many programs are open and how much memory your Mac has, switching accounts may cause small delays and increased drive activity.

To enable fast user switching, choose > System Preferences > Users & Groups > Login Options (click if the settings are dimmed). Turn on "Show fast user switching menu as". Use the pop-up menu to show the accounts menu as a user name or a compact icon .

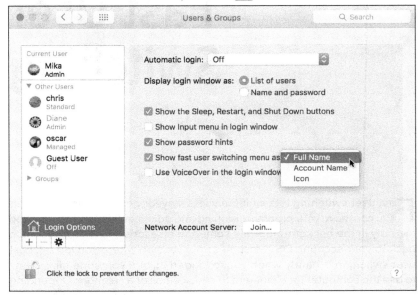

 To switch users, choose another user name from the accounts menu on the right side of the menu bar. This menu appears only when fast user switching is turned on and shows a check mark next to the name of each logged-in user. To be safe, save all work before switching (in case another logged-in user shuts down or restarts the computer).

If you try to shut the Mac down or restart it while other people are logged in, a dialog box tells you, "There are currently logged in users who may lose unsaved changes if you shut down this computer". You can click Cancel or you can type an administrator password and click Shut Down (shutting down all accounts open in the background and their open documents, possibly making enemies of the other users).

Tip: You can't make changes to accounts (in System Preferences) that are still logged in. You also can't turn off fast user switching or turn on FileVault while other people are logged in.

CHAPTER 10

OS X and Malware

Malware (malicious software) includes computer viruses, worms, trojan horses, ransomware, spyware, adware, scareware, and other hostile programs. Unlike malware-laden Windows, OS X has a strong reputation for security and stability, generally because:

- No OS X program (including malware) can install itself without your explicit permission and awareness. OS X notifies you when any program tries to install itself on your Mac. Every time that you download a program (executable code) file via Safari or Mail (even programs in a .zip file), a dialog box warns you that it might be harmful.

- System Integrity Protection (Chapter 17) prevents all users (even administrators) from modifying the contents of OS X's critical system folders. Malware might be able to erase or encrypt your personal files, but it wouldn't be able to access other users' files or the operating system itself.

- By default, OS X **ports** are closed. Ports are channels that remote computers use to pass data in and out of your computer. Open ports are fine and necessary for expected communications traffic. But an errant open port exposes your computer to attack (the 2003 Blaster worm infiltrated millions of Windows PCs via open ports, for example).

- The Erase feature (with Security Options) of Disk Utility can securely erase a drive by overwriting it with meaningless data multiple times, so that deleted files can't be undeleted with specialized data-recovery tools. You can also use the srm (secure remove) command in Terminal to delete files and folders securely.

- Safari's Private Browsing mode lets you visit websites without leaving any history, passwords, searches, cookies, or other digital breadcrumbs.

CHAPTER 11

Gatekeeper

O S X's **Gatekeeper** security feature helps prevent you from inadvertently installing viruses, spyware, and other malware. Gatekeeper works by restricting which downloaded apps you can install. To enable app installations (Gatekeeper), choose > System Preferences > Security & Privacy > General pane (click if the settings are dimmed).

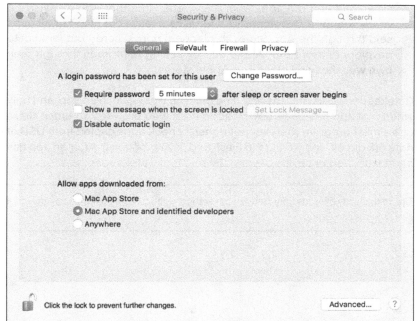

Under "Allow apps downloaded from", choose one of the following options:

Mac App Store

Download and run apps from only the Mac App Store. The App Store is the safest place to get apps because it's curated, meaning that Apple vets the developers and reviews their apps before accepting them to the store. If there's a problem with an app, Apple removes it from the store. Before you download and install an app, you can read reviews from other users.

Mac App Store and identified developers

Download and run App Store apps and non-App Store apps that have a Developer ID. Developers that register with Apple get a unique Developer ID, which they can use to digitally sign the apps that they create. This digital signature is cryptographically secure and lets Gatekeeper verify that the app hasn't been tampered with since it left the hands of the developer. Signed apps aren't necessarily sold through the App Store and aren't pre-screened by Apple, but if Apple discovers any problems with apps created by a registered developer, they can block that developer's apps and revoke their credentials. OS X updates its list of blacklisted developers once each day.

Anywhere

Download and run apps from anywhere. Note that Apple charges a yearly fee for a Developer ID and takes a large cut (30%) of all apps sold through the App Store, so plenty of unregistered but legitimate developers avoid the "Apple tax" by selling their apps through their own websites and other non-Apple stores.

Gatekeeper works only the first time that you try to launch an app, and only when that app has been downloaded via a web browser, an email client, or a similar program (Gatekeeper doesn't check apps copied from USB or network drives, and won't stop Flash and Java programs). After an app has been launched once, it's beyond the reach of Gatekeeper.

Tip: To manually override your Gatekeeper setting, right-click an unsigned app in Finder and then choose Open.

CHAPTER 12

FileVault

FileVault automatically encrypts and password-protects your entire drive (including external USB and FireWire drives). After you set up FileVault, it runs in the background. Everything works like before, with no noticeable performance hit, except now your data are secured against laptop thieves, drive thieves, cops, and customs agents at border crossings. Your files are readable by only you and anyone with a master recovery key. Any shared folders (Chapter 8) in your home folder become unreadable by others on the network when you're not logged in. Time Machine can copy an encrypted home folder only when you're logged out. FileVault uses standard XTS-AES 128 encryption; if you forget your password and the master recovery key, your data are lost forever.

Tip: To quickly encrypt a particular drive, right-click the drive icon in Finder or on the desktop and then choose Encrypt.

To set up FileVault, choose > System Preferences > Security & Privacy > FileVault pane (click 🔒 if the settings are dimmed). Click Turn On FileVault and then follow the onscreen instructions. During the process, an auto-generated key is added to the keychains of assigned users (Chapter 15), letting them unlock (decrypt) their FileVault-encrypted data by remember-ing only a login password (page 13). (Alternatively, you can use your iCloud password as the key.) You must give explicit permission to each user that you want to allow to log in to a FileVault-protected Mac. Any user with a passwordless account must set a password. Print, copy, or store the recovery key when it appears (in large type). The recovery key is a master password that lets an administrator access any account without knowing the account holder's password, or turn off FileVault for any account.

Tip: If FileVault is turned on, the Recovery HD partition won't appear when you hold down the Option key during startup, but you can still hold down Command+R during startup to boot directly to it.

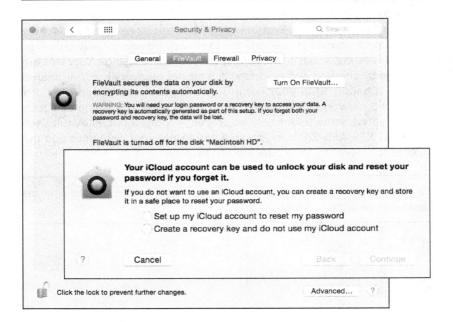

CHAPTER 13

Firewall

A **firewall** is a piece of software or hardware that helps screen out hackers and malware that try to reach your computer over the internet. It's the most important security component on your computer or network; if you don't have one, attackers can compromise your computer minutes after you go online. OS X provides Firewall for free, but consider using a router too.

A router is a small box that distributes the signal from your modem (DSL, cable, or dial-up) to the computers on your network. A router has a built-in firewall and appears to the outside world to be a computer without programs and hard drives to attack or infect; it's the safest type of firewall, because it protects your entire network and is always on. Even if you're not on a network, you can put a router between your computer and your modem. If you're on a network, a router won't protect you from *other* computers on the network if one of them becomes infected because someone downloaded a virus. For that kind of protection, you need OS X's software Firewall on your individual computer.

To turn Firewall on or off, choose ◉ > System Preferences > Security & Privacy > Firewall pane > Turn On/Off Firewall (click 🔒 if the settings are dimmed). Turn off Firewall only if you're using a router, a different firewall, or someone's shared internet connection.

Tip: To see the Firewall log, choose Applications > Utilities > Console > appfirewall.log (under /var/log).

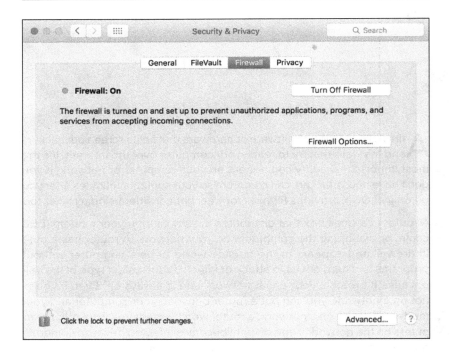

To configure Firewall, choose > System Preferences > Security & Privacy >
Firewall pane > Firewall Options (click 🔒 if the settings are dimmed), and
then set the following options:

Block all incoming connections
    Blocks everything but a few crucial network services (secure but
    limiting).

[List of services and applications]
    Blocks all incoming signals except those sent to programs that you've
    approved (the most flexible choice). In the list, OS X's sharing features
    appear automatically above the divider line. To add a program, click
    ☐+☐, choose the program, and then click ◇ to set its limits. To delete a
    program, select it and click ☐—☐.

Automatically allow signed software to receive incoming connections
    Trusts well-known programs whose authenticity has been confirmed
    by a third-party certificate authority.

Enable stealth mode
    Makes your Mac invisible to automated cracker programs trolling the
    internet. OS X won't respond to "pings" (including those from you when
    you're travelling).

CHAPTER 14

Password Assistant

Password Assistant helps you avoid creating easily guessed passwords (names, birthdays, dictionary words, and so on). It can generate secure passwords or rate ones that you make up. To open Password Assistant, click 🔑 wherever you're supposed to create a password—in Users & Groups (Chapter 3) or Keychain Access (Chapter 15), for example. To test your own password, type it in the Suggestion box; otherwise, use the Type pop-up menu and the Length slider to generate secure passwords. (FIPS-181 is a standard U.S. government password-generating algorithm.) The Quality bar shows password toughness.

Tip: Thanks to the Keychain Access password-memorizer, you don't have to remember any passwords other than your account login password.

Password Assistant		
Type:	Memorable	
Suggestion:	ATVs12*stung	
Length:		12
Quality:		
Tips:		

CHAPTER 15

Keychain Access

Use Keychain Access to manage your passwords for secure websites, FTP sites, network servers, encrypted folders and volumes, and other secure items. OS X creates, maintains, and unlocks your default (login) keychain automatically, so passwords are available when they're needed to access secured items and locations. You can also store credit-card numbers, PINs, and other private data in secure notes on your keychain. Keychain Access remembers passwords only for programs that are keychain-aware.

To open Keychain Access: Choose Applications > Utilities > Keychain Access.

To add a keychain item: Access a secure item or location normally, type your password when prompted, and then choose to save or remember the password (you may have to click an Options button). The password is added to your keychain and appears in Keychain Access.

Tip: To make Safari remember your login credentials for various websites in your keychain, open Safari, choose Safari > Preferences > AutoFill tab, and then select "User names and passwords". From now on, Safari will fill in saved user names and passwords automatically when you log in to memorized websites.

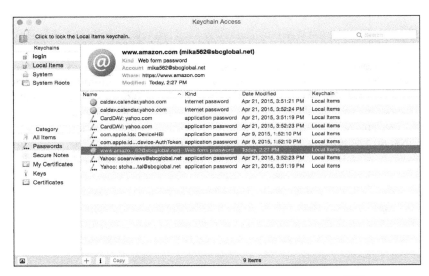

To add a password item manually: In Keychain Access, click ⊞ or choose File > New Password Item (Command+N). Type a name or URL in the Keychain Item Name box. Type a user ID or account name or number in the Account Name box. Type the password in the Password box (select Show Typing to reveal your password as you type, or click 🔑 for password help; see Chapter 14). When you're done, click Add.

To add a secure note: In Keychain Access, choose File > New Secure Note Item (Shift+Command+N). Type a name for the note in the Keychain Item Name box. Type the note in the Note box. When you're done, click Add.

To delete a keychain item: In Keychain Access, select the target item and then choose Edit > Delete or press Delete.

To inspect or control access to a keychain item: In Keychain Access, double-click the item, or select it and click ⓘ . To see the text of password or secure note, click the Attributes tab and then select "Show password" or "Show note".

To control access to the item, click the Access Control tab and then choose one of the following options:

Allow all applications to access this item
Lets any program access the item, without showing a confirmation dialog box.

Confirm before allowing access
Shows a confirmation dialog box for every program that tries to access the item. "Ask for Keychain password" determines whether the confirmation prompts for a password. Use $\boxed{+}\,\boxed{-}$ to add or delete programs that can access the item without triggering the confirmation.

Click Save Changes, type the keychain password in the dialog box that appears, and then click Allow.

To use a keychain item: Access a secure item or location normally. If Access Control permits access to the item without confirmation, the item opens without showing a confirmation dialog box; otherwise, click one of the following buttons in the confirmation dialog box:

Always Allow
Lets the keychain open the item and adds the item to the Access Control list to suppress this dialog box in the future.

Deny
Prevents use of the keychain item; type a password to access the secure item.

Allow
Lets the keychain open the item this time.

To manage keychains: To create a new keychain, choose File > New Keychain (Option+Command+N). To view a different keychain, click ▣ to show the Keychains list and then click the keychain. To lock or unlock a keychain, select it and then click the lock at the top of the Keychain Access window. Keychains are stored as files in ~/Library/Keychains (~ denotes your home folder). You can copy these files to other Macs.

CHAPTER 16

Privacy Settings

To set miscellaneous privacy-related options, choose > System Preferences > Security & Privacy > Privacy pane (click 🔒 if the settings are dimmed).

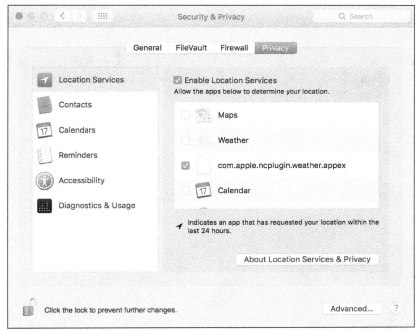

Location Services
> Location Services lets apps and services use your physical whereabouts via the Mac's built-in positioning service, which determines your

approximate location by using the data from nearby wireless hotspots. For example, Location Services lets your laptop determine its own time zone automatically, lets Maps determine your current location, and lets a weather website show your local weather the first time that you visit the site. The first time an app makes a request to use Location Services, OS X opens a location warning for that app, which you can allow or block. Your response sticks, and the request isn't shown again. You can turn off Location Services for some or for all apps and services.

Contacts, Calendars, Reminders
Choose which apps and services can access your contacts, calendars, and reminders.

Twitter, Facebook, LinkedIn
Choose which apps and services can access your social networking accounts (if you've created those accounts in > System Preferences > Internet Accounts).

Accessibility
Choose which apps and services can control your computer's Accessibility features.

Diagnostics & Usage
If you select these checkboxes, your Mac will quietly and automatically send anonymous data to Apple and third-party developers (via Apple) about your crashes, freezes, programs, hardware, peripherals, and so on. Don't bother; save the bandwidth.

CHAPTER 17

Other Security Measures

Secure Virtual Memory

If you're running a lot of programs and hit the limits of physical memory (RAM), OS X claims drive space and creates a **swap file** to use as virtual memory. By default, OS X encrypts swap files so that thieves can't pluck data and passwords off your drive. (In old OS X versions, you had to turn on secure virtual memory manually.)

System Integrity Protection

System Integrity Protection, also called "rootless", prevents the user or any process from modifying the contents of system-protected folders, including /System, /bin, /sbin, and /usr (except for /usr/local). Not even administrators can add to these folders or edit files that they contain, though they retain their access to the rest of the files on the drive. In Terminal, you can't use the sudo command in protected directories.

This feature makes Macs more resistant to attacks and malware, but it also limits what advanced users can do to their systems. To circumvent System Integrity Protection, restart your Mac, hold down the Option key during startup, and then choose Recovery HD when the list of startup partitions appears. In the Utilities menu, toggle System Integrity Protection.

Tip: To check the status of System Integrity Protection, run the command `csrutil status` in Terminal.

Two-Factor Authentication

Two-factor authentication is a robust, optional security add-on for your Apple ID on OS X and iOS. When this feature is turned on, an enemy needs not only your password to break in, but also access to another of your devices. When you sign in to a new device or web browser with your Apple ID, you must verify your identity by typing your Apple ID password *and* a separate six-digit verification code. This code displays automatically on all the other OS X (El Capitan or later) and iOS (version 9 or later) devices that you're currently signed in to. Type the code on the new device.

You don't need to verify a device again unless you erase it, change your password, or remove it from your Apple ID's trusted device list. To see this list on your Mac, choose > System Preferences > iCloud > Account Details > Devices tab.

To set up two-factor authentication on your Mac, choose > System Preferences > iCloud > Account Details > Security tab > Set Up Two-Factor Authentication.

For details, read the Apple support article "Two-factor authentication for Apple ID" at *support.apple.com/ht204915*.

Tip: Two-factor authentication is built into OS X 10.11 (El Capitan) and later and iOS 9 and later. If you already set up your devices to use Apple's older two-step verification process on earlier versions of OS X and iOS, then you can continue to use that older process. (Two-factor authentication isn't the same process as two-step verification.)

Index